BRITAIN'S STORY:
AN OVERVIEW OF
BRITISH HISTORY

ERIC MIDWINTER

For Sylvia
All good wishes
Eric Midwinter

June 2013.

Third Age Press

Third Age Press

ISBN 978-1-898576-31-9
First edition

Third Age Press Ltd, 2012
Third Age Press, 6 Parkside Gardens
London SW19 5EY
Managing Editor Dianne Norton

© Eric Midwinter

Cover & layout design by Dianne Norton
Printed by Rushmere Printers London

THIRD AGE PRESS

. . . a unique publishing company . . . an independent publishing company which recognizes that the period of life after full-time employment and family responsibility can be a time of fulfilment and continuing development . . . a time of regeneration

Third Age Press books are available by direct mail order from **Third Age Press,** 6 Parkside Gardens London SW19 5EY

or on order through bookshops or from Amazon

Email: dnort@globalnet.co.uk

Website: www.thirdagepress.co.uk – for full list of publications or send SAE for catalogue

CONTENTS

What the critics say

(Francis Becket, *History Today* April 2013)

Midwinter succeeds because he is a social historian. He doesn't worry if he misses out a king or several, because he knows he's giving his readers the overarching trends that show us how our society developed. He offers illuminating information that a conventional politician or literary writer might have left out, such as how the size of Britain's population rose and fell and what this tells us about the nation was feeling.

And there are shafts of insight. In the years from 1066 to 1216, '*the ordinary folk went stolidly about their business of farming the land while their purported superiors indulged in extravagant and wounding political activities*'. Much later, after he has demonstrated – as someone with more space could not have done – that Britain's empire '*vanished within 100 years, making it one of the most short lived of all history's many Empires*', Midwinter reminds us how keen Britain's politicians still are to disport themselves if not intrude themselves on the world stage: '*It was as if Britain could not adjust to the displeasing model of being a larger version of Denmark, with a sound economy backed by excellent public service*'.

Eric Midwinter is a historian of comedy and cricket, an expert in education and in ageing (he's 80 this year) and one of the three founders of the University of the Third Age, a lifelong learning co-operative for older people no longer in full-time work. Only such a person could have produced this tremendous little book.

BRITAIN'S STORY: FOREWORD

This an attempt to offer adults with a general interest in national history a concise summary of that 2000 year epic. It is hopefully designed to enable some to arrange random, vague gobbets of information in orderly fashion and to whet the appetite of others to read further.

It is customary to look back chronologically at history from the current standpoint with less recent events diminished and more recent events magnified. When the writer started secondary school in the 1940s his first year history primer, and a most interesting one it was too, was called *Flints to Printing*. It covered well over 1500 years. The magisterial and indispensable *The Oxford History of England* began with a volume on Roman Britain, covering some 500 years, and ended with a volume on the period 1914 to 1945, just 31 years.

This brief narrative endeavours to provide more of an overview, looking down rather than back and seeing events against a more natural time pattern, trying to judge the relative significance of happenings over the same temporal perspective. It is by no means a complete break with the old proportions of attention to particular periods but it does travel quite some way in that direction. The summary is in six chapters. The first two – on Roman Britain and on the Barbarian Settlement – cover the first thousand years; the third and fourth sections deal with medieval Britain, a matter of about 500 years, while modern Britain, from about 1485, is split fairly evenly over the last 500 years.

It does mean that, with a very concise text and a concentration on events that played an important part in the evolution of today's Britain, there are some changes of emphasis from the normal historical record. For example, the 1530s, when primary decisions were made about the nature of the centralised British nation-state, looms into a more accented reckoning, with Thomas Cromwell assuming as much apparent import as Oliver Cromwell. The year 1641, when the elements were thrashed out of the constitutional monarchy that is still the base of British governance, has more attention paid to it than the struggle it led to in the subsequent years of dramatic and colourful action. Because of the decision to take a more equitable view of the time frame, the coverage of the 20th century may look particularly squashed, even dismissive. The 1914-1918 and 1939-1945 World Wars, for instance, the memories and experiences of which informed the daily lives of recent generations, seam together as scenes in the havoc of a war-torn century.

The moral may lie in acknowledging that our predecessors enjoyed, if they were lucky, a similar time-span. We know that, at least since 1066, something like 5 to 10% of British inhabitants lived to be over sixty. They would have personally witnessed much the same length of 'history' as their descendants today, whether it was a phase of woe or unrest caused by the Black Death, the English Civil War or World Wars I and II or maybe a more peaceable phase. Every life, on immediate criteria, is just as vastly important and, against the canvas of 2000 years, just as minuscule in impact as any other. And the same applies to each passage of history from the sparse few gathered around the Iron Age encampments to the crowded many in the confused tempo of early 21st century Britain.

Chapter 1
THE RISE AND FALL OF ROMAN BRITAIN
55BC – 440

Britain's recorded history, where, that is, there is some documentary as well as archaeological record, covers some two thousand years, from the arrival of the Romans to the present day. It is a lengthy period – and the Roman episode occupies a quarter of that time.

Nonetheless it is a relatively brief span of humankind's story, let alone that of the planet humankind inhabits. Were the history of the earth to be represented by the scale model of one calendar year, the Roman invasion of Britain would have taken place at one minute to midnight on the 31st December of that year. The human species would have arrived on the scene about 11.30 on that same evening. It is salutary to have some sense of the wider perspective when studying the history of a specific period.

Moreover, there had been plenty of human activity in Britain before the advent of the Romans. There had been hunters and gatherers in the British Isles for thousands of years, for 33,000 years according to some sources. In the times of hunters, gatherers and fishers, populations were small, for it has been calculated that, on average, one square kilometre of usable land – think 200 football pitches – would have been needed to support one person. Thus, say, about 8000 BC, the British population would have been about 5000, with the corollary that the family groups may well have survived with little or no contact among them.

About 3000 BC, Neolithic peoples migrated into Britain from the continent, introducing stock raising, tillage and other agrarian methods. The agricultural revolution was perhaps the greatest breakthrough in human history. It allowed for settlement and the other trappings of what we term 'civilisation'. Stonehenge probably dates from about that time, indicating a degree of technical and cultural sophistication. Pre-Roman Britain was nothing like the cartoon version of cave-dwelling, woad-wearing Ancient Britons of uncouth habit and savage mien. The inhabitants of these islands had pursued a path through the Neolithic and Bronze stages, and into the Iron Age, with, for instance, considerable evidence of Iron Age forts. The Romans found social and cultural practices at one with those they had encountered throughout much of north-western Europe. In particular, the Belgae tribes, who inhabited part of Gaul, exported, by migration and by imitation, substantial elements of the Belgic culture to Britain. By language and culture, the early Britons fell largely into what might loosely be termed the Celtic fold – and this Celtic substratum was to be maintained in the outer fringes of Britain that the Romans were never able to tame.

It was a largely tribal culture of a warrior upper class backed by agricultural labour, and the Celtic tribes were not immune to quarrelsomeness. For all that, there were, in pre-Roman times, several familiar routes between the south of England and the continent. The first recognition – British history presents many – that this was never a 'tight little right little island' but a region constantly open to strong overseas influence. One of the reasons the Romans decided to conquer the British Isles was because of the assistance given by British-based tribes to their fellows in Gallic territories.

In itself this was but one aspect of the wider sense in which Britain was drawn, from these beginnings of its recorded history, into very close ties with the continent. The massive Roman Empire had grown, in part, through a series of defensive measures, constantly creating buffers around areas already occupied. The stoppage of British support of Gallic uprisings was one of the last of these endeavours. Trade was equally important – and the mineral and grain exports available from Britain were considerable. Then there was the sheer politics of Roman ambition, with generals – such as Julius Caesar and his Gallic victories – seeking the kind of military glory that was the necessary stepping stone to power.

The visits of Julius Caesar in 55 and 54BC touched on all these aspects but they were transient affairs. He certainly imposed friendly rulers on, and extorted an annual tribute or tax from, some of the southern tribes, but it was felt there was no need for formal occupation. The significance lay more in his sighting of Britain for future reference. He had crossed the tidal 'ocean' of the Channel, disliked by Romans used to the calm of the Mediterranean, and revealed what had been remote islands on the misty edge of the world as something of value and interest. Practical lessons had been learned with difficulty. The precedent had been set – but it was to be nearly a century before another serious move was made.

It was Claudius who picked up the gauntlet in 43AD. Thrust unceremoniously into power and of unknown repute, some overseas triumph was essential to the furtherance of his imperial reign. Hostile reaction to the Roman oversight and taxation of Britain was his excuse. He was fortunate in as much as the Roman army was at its peak of meticulous organisation. It provided a profession both for Roman citizens and for aspiring subjects of Roman colonies, known as 'auxiliaries'. The army included a wide range of opportunities for trades and clerical skills. The pay, unusually for pre-modern armies, was regular. Even more unusually, the literacy levels were in consequence, very high, and both serving and retired soldiers were well thought of and well treated.

A legion consisted of some 5000 men, mostly heavy infantry, backed by auxiliaries recruited in regiments of 500 men. For instance, when, later, the route-way between the great forts of Deva (Chester) and Ebor (York) had to be patrolled, it was the 1st Cohort Freisian Auxiliaries, detached from the XXth Legion at Deva, who garrisoned the encampment at Mancunium (Manchester). Four legions and much the same number of auxiliaries – 40,000 personnel in total – comprised the invading force. The British warrior aristocracy, with their chariots, led the defence, accompanied by levies summoned from the farms. Technically they were no match, especially in pitched battle, for the well-armed and heavily protected Roman troops, and the wonder is that resistance was fiercely upheld for so long.

Gradually, the south and east of Britain was occupied. All the lands as far as the Severn and the Trent were in Roman hands by 47AD. Governmental mechanics were soon instituted, often using client tribal kings, but with Rome dispatching reliable and competent administrators to supervise the occupation – it was a feather in one's cap to receive a British posting. Exports, such as silver from the Mendips mines, were soon streaming back to Rome. Agriculture was also well developed in Britain, another source for trade. It is now believed that Britain was much less forested than had once been estimated. Archaeological evidence suggests amazingly that a cultivated landscape had already emerged in pre-Roman Britain with a framework of land division similar to the present day.

Town life grew. Colchester was the first base of note but the port of London soon grew in prestige. As so frequently happened, the perils of border raids to the west and north compelled the Romans to press beyond their original and natural river boundaries and for some time the building of roads and townships continued steadily.

However, there was unease within the initial Roman domain, with harsh injustice and negligent maladministration the cause, as it was so often throughout the Roman realm. Famously, Boudica, in 60AD, led her own tribe, the Iceni, and their allies, the Trinovantes, in a fiery revolt against the Roman occupier. She swept through Southern Britain, burning Colchester, London and Verulamium (St Albans) in devastating style. The whole province was at risk, but the Roman authorities restored some semblance of order with equal severity.

It took time to recover from this rebellion and to recommence the building programme of urban development and roadways.

This was the chief example of what was to characterise the Roman occupation of Britain. Passages of peaceful activity with the accent on economic growth alternated with periods of marked unrest, either internally or from the tribes on the extensive frontiers of the occupied territories. The post-Boudica re-conquest of British territory by the Romans was fairly decisive and was followed by an era of urban construction. The 'civitates' or governmental areas all had administrative centres, replete with leisure and allied amenities, including public baths and engineered water supplies. Some towns, such as Lincoln and Gloucester, were mainly allocated to retired soldiers. There was also the spread of the 'villa' life for both Roman visiting officials and well-to-do native Britons. Their relatively isolated locations indicated there was sufficient reliance on good order to make the 'villa' life-style viable. A feature of these developments was the participation of the local aristocracies in administration and the building of towns as well as in the ownership of villas. All this pointed to a more complete Romanisation of Britain, as the characteristic Roman process of persuading the leading lights of the indigenous population to adopt Roman ways and practices was pursued. In religious observance, the Celts and Romans both found congenial the animistic notion of localised deities and their ritualistic worship.

Nonetheless, there was always some unease, principally at the fringes. The Romans had occupied most of Scotland but fierce opposition forced them to settle for what became the traditional Scottish border, magnificently marked by Hadrian's Wall, the construction of which began in 122, and a fortification that, it is thought, acted not only as a defensive barrier but as a control filter for goods and people. Despite two or three further major assaults, Scotland never again fell under the Roman heel, while Wales too, was never wholly brought under Roman control.

The see-saw continued. Whether Britain was subject to central Roman command or to more regional arrangements and whether its domestic economy was stable or not, depended largely on the political conditions of the Empire itself. The constant internecine squabbles that disabled the overall integrity of the Roman state obviously affected

Britain, an area regarded as both an asset and a prize by the Roman hierarchy.

The last and the most important of these disputes began at York, when the army proclaimed Constantine, son of the Emperor Constantine I, as Caesar (306-337). Building on the improved conditions of the last decades of the 3rd century, Britain enjoyed a prosperous half century thereafter. Much was due to the favourable interest of Constantine, a man who ruled on the grand scale. There was a flowering of the 'villa' culture, always a sign of reasonable good order, with a rich Romano-British aristocracy, an amalgam of the still surviving Celtic families of noble blood and the senior officials despatched from Rome. These often immense residences, with coal or wood fuelled hot air heating systems and usually with adjoining agricultural estates, have been likened, in opulent comfort and in political clout, with Hanoverian country houses. Although there seems to have been some tendency toward the kind of manorial village life prominent in medieval times, the agrarian system was still mainly based on scattered small farms cultivated by Britons.

Administratively, the 'diocese' of Britain, with its headquarters definitively located in London, was subdivided into four provinces, probably based on London, Lincoln, York and Cirencester. Their officers were responsible for the civil governance of these areas and they also had the important task of providing the army with supplies. British officialdom was subordinate to the Gallic prefecture at Trier, then a major base in Roman political affairs.

Constantine's pre-eminent and long-term contribution to British and European history was his decision to legitimise Christianity. The 313 Edict of Milan, by insisting on tolerance for the Christian faith, halted the persecution of what was a tiny minority, so that with his sanction and encouragement, Christianity became overnight tantamount to the official religion of the Empire. There is much debate as to the extent his motives were pragmatic or sincere, but the upshot of his insistence on orthodoxy and the right and necessity of the Emperor and, by extension, other rulers to determine what faith his subjects should hold was to have manifest and sometimes calamitous consequences over the fullness of time.

As for Britain, Christianity had been patchy, although it had had its martyrs, such as St Alban. Henceforward it thrived, as elsewhere in the Empire. The pagan cults suffered from the absence of imperial backing and from the removal of endowments into Christian hands. In many of the towns and among the villa culture, especially where landowners or officials were either enthusiastic for the faith or simply ambitious, and thus requiring to be identified with the Christian cause, Christianity flourished.

All in all, the time just before, during and immediately after Constantine, was a brief golden age for Roman Britain. It was the pleasant calm before the violent storm.

The decline and fall of the Roman Empire took, as Charles II legendarily said when apologising for his tardy death, 'an unquestionably long time'. It is perhaps a truism to say that until the entire force of the catastrophe struck, the Romans did not realise it was happening. No one has the prior gift of hindsight. However, in this case the symptoms of deterioration had been witnessed so commonly over the centuries of Roman dominion that it must have been difficult to spot the incremental difference that tipped the balance.

On the one hand, subject tribes and kingdoms did not always remain cowed and those on the borders of the Empire often embarked on offensive forays. On the other hand, dissension in the body politic of Rome was not unusual, with fierce in-fighting the corrosive norm, often with added problems of reduced military zeal or over-weighty bureaucratic inertia. Over a hundred year period, perhaps longer, the interaction of these two elements became more compelling. At the risk of some simplification the Barbarians sensed the weakness of the Empire and redoubled their assaults and uprisings, which in turn, further enfeebled the Roman hierarchy, leading to renewed pressure from ever more buoyant Barbarian tribes. There were other factors, such as the stress some tribes close to or within the imperial boundaries were placed under by attacks upon them by their immediate neighbours, but the interaction of stronger Barbarian and weaker Roman institutions was at the hub of Rome's downfall.

Once again, Britain provides a microcosmic view of that whole picture. In the middle of the fourth century, Britain was caught up in one of those maelstroms of political unrest and was severely damaged by oppressive measures, including exile, executions and the confiscation of property. Civilians and military alike were demoralised and dismayed, and there was consequent crumbling of the economic and organisational fabric. The Scots from Ireland and the Picts from Scotland were not slow to take advantage and, in 367, they carried out surprise raids, cleverly synchronised with attacks on Gaul by the Saxons and Franks. The invaders enjoyed much success. They roamed England unchecked and even occupied London.

It took the arrival of a small but elite army, probably composed in part of skilled Barbarian mercenaries, to turn the tide on an assault that had reeked havoc throughout most of what was now five Roman provinces. It was a thorough success and over the rest of the century garrisons were restored, town life was enhanced, ports were strengthened, the bureaucracy was enlarged and, in main part, stability and prosperity was regained. Superficially, it seemed that Roman efficiency had overcome the by no means uncommon forays of dangerous Barbarian war-parties.

The early fifth century saw renewed problems. The power of Roman authority was very much undermined and Barbarian invasions struck deep into the heartlands of Roman dominion. It appears that Roman troops were withdrawn to defend the Empire elsewhere but in 409, Romano-British forces succeeded in repelling Saxon attacks and, dissatisfied with the fractious character and increasing ineffectiveness of Roman rule, the British took the fundamental decision to break off relations with what was by now a dislocated and collapsing Roman system.

There was a slight possibility of Roman military intervention but given the other stressful demands on Rome's defences it never happened. For some decades, and in so far as the Barbarians remained amenable, there was a post-Roman interval during which, for all the poor effects on the artisan and middle classes, the well-to-do gentry and their like, of both Roman and British stock, existed in reasonable comfort.

Soon the expeditions of the Angles and Saxons and Jutes would bring basic changes, and almost half a millennium of Romanisation would be at an end. Obviously, so prolonged and intense a spell of occupation would leave a genuine mark. Britain is today scattered with the architectural debris and remains of walls, fortifications, amphitheatres and other relics of Romano-British life. Urban sites and route-ways still owe much to Roman precedents and origins, although these, to some extent, are predetermined by geographical dictates and may have blossomed in the same manner under other or later human initiatives. Culturally speaking, the Roman legitimisation of Christianity and its more formal introduction into Britain was to be of enormous import to the history of this country.

This makes for a large legacy, but in other regards the Roman heritage may seem less potent than one would expect from 500 years of settlement. This possibly arose from the very nature of the switch from Roman to Barbarian control. Population is often a useful guide. At the peak of its splendour, during the Constantinian era of the fourth century, the population of Roman Britain may have been as much as 4m – two to three times as much as it was when the Domesday survey was completed soon after the Norman Conquest. It seems certain that the population decline began in the last decades before the advent of the conquering Barbarian invaders. Thus it was that the general principle of ancient Rome's demise – a lame and broken land proved tempting to evermore confident and tough-minded immigrants – proved decisive. In those last years troops and officials and presumably their families moved away or fled; perhaps some native British groups retreated to the fastnesses of the Celtic fringes and almost certainly there was that drop in population which afflicts every community under social duress.

As well as inheriting a much less virile society, the Anglo-Saxons were by their own lights adverse to Roman ways, eschewing, for example, Roman towns and the pleasures of urban life. They made little or no effort, as some other Barbarian tribes had done, to adopt Roman institutions and values, and this attitude, coupled with the relatively frail presence of Roman influence when they arrived, ensured that a kind of social vacuum was created. Although much that was Roman endured, much was, for better or for worse, lost.

Chapter 2
THE ANGLO-SAXON AND DANISH SETTLEMENT
440 – 1066

It is seldom realised that the combine of the Roman occupation of Britain and the subsequent settlement of the Anglo-Saxon and Danish migrants fills a half of the beaker of recorded British history. Enduring from just before the birth of Jesus to the beginnings of the second millennium, these two major events occupied a thousand years of British history. It is natural to seek for a defining characteristic or two to identify with each historical episode, with, in these two cases, the former Roman period often regarded as one of some stability and peace, and the latter English settlement seen as one of warring and upset. People speak of the Pax Romana versus the Dark Ages.

The difficulty of stereotyping half a millennium is obvious enough. Just as, in any analysis of Roman Britain, the prevalence of native rebellion, internecine squabbling among the occupiers and intrusive Barbarian assaults must be emphasised as well as the phases of peace and prosperity, so is it true to note in the second half of the first millennium a similar mix of events. Certainly the waves of Barbarian incursion must take some main degree of priority in any such examination, but one should also recall the lengthy times and many areas when life was relatively peaceful and free from political strife. That said, the dominating strands of this epoch were indeed the three great tides of incoming groups. First came the Angles, Saxons and Jutes at the beginning of the period; next to arrive were the Vikings or Danish invaders part way through this era, and then at the last, there was the Norman-French conquest midway through the 11th century.

Two preliminary points should be made. In the first place, these were not isolated assaults on a lonely target. The whole of the Roman Empire was beset by distress and anxiety as swarms of tribes moved, migrated and fought their way across and around the old imperial realms. In one sense, there was nothing novel about this. Throughout the time of Rome's domination there had been, as Britain itself had demonstrated, uprisings against the Roman occupation, along with some nomadic or martial movement among the tribes. The Romans for instance, never completely or for long settled what was to become Scotland. Nonetheless, the sheer weight and intensity of such activity became sufficient to mark it off as a change in kind rather than degree.

There were varied reasons for this, including factors such as rising population and resultant land-hunger, together with Barbarian tribes, especially to the east of Europe and beyond, such as the Tartars, pressing one upon the other. In the particular case of Britain, it is thought that rising sea-levels and flooding on the Baltic coast lands may well have added to the need for new land. A major reason, of course, was the weakening of the Empire itself, its years of maintaining order over vast tracts of land contributing to the general malaise of military and political fatigue. An interaction of weakening Romanisation and strengthening Barbarianism evolved. The departure of Roman troops from Britain is just one instance of that gradual process of lowered sustenance on the part of the Romans and of heightened confidence on the part of the Barbarians. It is believed that, by this juncture,the Roman grasp on British life and customs was quite fragile.

In the second place, the generic term 'the Barbarian Invasions' does, for all its basic truth, require a little exegesis. Because of the fears of the Romans and because of the actual mayhem caused by them, the term 'Barbarian' took on a wholly negative connotation for wild and uncivilised behaviour, with the Huns, Goths, Tartars and Vandals adding specialised contributions to that interpretation. However, the root for the word for Barbarian is more strictly construed as stranger or incomer. Several of these tribes were not as black as they have been painted. Some were quite advanced . History is constantly discovering that the peoples of bygone eras were often not so uncultivated as had been imagined – the cave-dwelling woad-painted British savage is an example.

That touches on the word 'invasions', with its flavour of military action. Again, these were often invasions in that sense, but they rarely led to purely military occupation. Much more so than in Roman times, these great movements were fundamentally domestic, in that, in pursuit of or even instead of martial success, women and children were quickly settled into new homes and onto new lands. There is evidence that their original homesteads were sometimes deserted, so comprehensive was the degree of migration.

The Venerable Bede, based in his monastery at Jarrow, completed in 711, his masterly *Ecclesiastical History of the English People*, in which he told of how the Germanic tribes of the Angles, Saxons and Jutes formed the first English settlements. They probably hailed from the areas of Angeln, Saxony and Jutland, but the chief factor is that they represented a wide-ranging culture spread across what now would be described as Northern France, Germany and southern Scandinavia. Once again there is a sense of the Germanic English belonging to a wider society; 'Britain exchanged the Roman Empire', it has been concluded, 'for another, if very different, international community'.

The 'Angle' and 'Saxon' influence persists in regional titles. East Anglia is one instance, together with the East, South and West Saxon derivation of Essex, Sussex and Wessex. As for the actual settlements, these were very much dictated by kin-group patterns and the intense strength of family bonds. These determined the allocation and usage of land and also the basis of the legal system, with retribution, such as the wergild or payment, sought by a victim's family. Loyalty to the kin-group and to the chiefs and lords of the tribes was a complementary feature.

The potency of kin-ship and its 'affinities' is demonstrated by place-names. 'Ing' refers to people or folk, as in Reading, the people of Reada, and by extension to the Darlington or Birmingham typology of endings. These often designated the lands held by one man and his many dependants, although these early settlements were not urban in any economic sense, referring more to the hierarchical focus of the relevant kin-group or family. A rural and farming people, the Anglo-Saxons barely utilised the old fortified and commercialised Roman places. They used the word 'ceaster' for these, hence the common incidence among English place-names of Dor(chester), Don(caster) or Lei(cester).

As for the native Romano-Britons, their numbers fell considerably – through flight, through disease and through that wasting of population than seems to attend the shattering of any society. Much of what is now England, including all of lowland England, was settled by the

German colonists, leaving Wales as the principal remaining British conclave, with Scotland still in the hands of the Picts, albeit with the growing Irish kingdom of Dalriada in the west, while the south-west of England formed the British kingdom of Dumnonia.

Indeed, kingdoms were all the rage in both the lands colonised by the Germanic tribes and those still held by the Romano-British and Celtic peoples. Although the familiar names of the larger kingdoms, such as Wessex, Kent or Northumbria are well recognised, the situation as of the end of the 6th century was much more fluid. In a condition of flux there could have been scores of kings in Britain at this time. Political life was uncertain and dangerous; there was feuding and much concentration on military might. The image of the kingly hall of Saxon days, with the king and his attendant 'thegns', that is, his sub-set of the military aristocracy, resting and feasting, seeking security from the perils abroad, remains a powerful one. And, as the Sutton Hoo royal burial site, uncovered by archaeologists in the 1930s on the east coast, testified, kingly largesse could be magnificent. The Beowulf epic conveys much of this heroic and sometimes ostentatious life-style

As if in counterpoint to the risks and anxieties of the political and military world, there was a curiously sane and rational substructure of administrative continuity in early Anglo-Saxon times. Its origins could have lain in Romano-British survival or it could have been introduced or invented by the Germanic settlers. It amounted to a very widespread system of division into 'hundreds', pieces of land of up to about a hundred square miles in area. Each contained a royal manor house as its depot – hence 'Kingston' and other such place-names – where the local people paid their dues in kind, with assessments based on 'hides' of land, and where, in turn, they sought protection and legal guarantees. What must be stressed is the very scattered nature of economic and social life. There was little of the bustling activity of the Roman town, still less the well-integrated community of the later medieval manor or village. Farming was, of course, the basis of the economy, but it was a relatively isolated affair, with smallholders, rather like ranchers in the 19th century American west, cultivating their land and tending their beasts on a largely individualistic base. The 'hundred' system suited this type of peasant economy. By the 7th century there were signs of the future manorial unit, but, for the most part, even such communities as existed lacked the kind of orderly plan that one would naturally associate with the typical village.

Among the Romano-British features that suffered was Christianity. At best a delicate plant, the tough pagan breezes of the Germanic culture caused it to shrivel. Where it did not perish, it retired into the remoteness of the British outer areas, where it survived, notably hidden away in scores of usually quite small monasteries. St Patrick's mission in 6th century Ireland was the outstanding achievement of this Celtic branch of Christianity. The alternative worship of the great Norse gods is most easily illustrated in their continuing celebration – Tiw, Woden, Thor – in our weekdays.

Once more, however, the strength of international influence prevailed. The Christian conversion began in 597, when Pope Gregory the Great sent the Roman monk, Augustine, to Kent, keen to play on the fact that King Aethelbert of Kent had a Christian queen, There were early successes, including Augustine's foundation of a monastery at Canterbury, thereby destined to be the headquarters of the English church. The conversion made only moderate progress initially. What might seem the tiny issue of the date of Easter was a sticking point in relations with the Celtic churches but the Synod of Whitby in 664 settled the matter in favour of the Roman church and henceforward it was the more cosmopolitan faith of Rome that was in the ascendant. Indeed, by the 8th century it was English churchmen who were refreshing the staleness of the Frankish church, with Alcuin, pupil of the York cathedral school, the central scholar of the Carolingian Renaissance associated with the powerful court of Charlemagne.

The lengthy archbishopric of Theodore in the last decades of the 7th century was something of an administrative turning-point. The impressive list of monasteries built and the completion of a diocesan system of government bear witness to his ability. Over the next fifty or so years there was an equally sound development of parochial oversight, with pastoral care for the peasantry supported by tithes, and the whole approved of by the kings. This testified to the mutual benefits that rulers and churchmen gained from the acceptance of a unified religion. It was because of this that Bede was able to entitle his seminal work the 'ecclesiastical' account of the English people.

The government of the one mirrored the government of the other, especially at local levels, while the educated clergy introduced much more literate elements into law making and judicial processes. Kings became less battle-hardened chiefs and more responsible governors.

Interestingly, the first clearly English towns were religious foundations, built about the great cathedrals and minsters, by far the most sophisticated organisms in English society.

In time trade which had international repercussions was rejuvenated. With this came the first instances of a new urban response, often with the suffix 'wic', derived from the Latin 'victus', meaning 'village' or more precisely, 'quarter', in the sense of a sector of a town, being used for commerce, with Ipswich and Sandwich as examples. Alongside the church and commerce, a further source of urban development was the fortress. This was especially true when the Viking invasions began, but, at places like Hereford and Bedford, there is evidence of earlier 'burhs' or fortified assemblages, built by Anglo-Saxon kings or lords for their own internal defence.

This touches on the contradiction, even the mild paradox, at the heart of the Anglo-Saxon structure. Whereas the lowly administrative levels were uniform and regulated, the top levels were subject to shifting fortunes. The English kingdoms, such as Mercia, Northumbria and Wessex, suffered from consistent dynastic troubles and inter-regional instability. There were often uncertainties about the succession, which was rarely direct, with candidates emerging from the royal stock and attempting to make good their claim. Although, chiefly through the vehicle of the church, there was a growing sense of an English culture, there was little evidence of an English polity.

In the era prior to the Viking invasions, the strongest monarch was Offa, king of Mercia from 757 to 796 – quite a lengthy reign for those times – one that brought Mercia closer to dominance over the English territories than any other competitor. Offa certainly styled himself 'king of the English' and he certainly acquired some temporary protective overlordship of Wessex. On the other hand, Northumbria remained autonomous. At best, Offa ruled over middle and southern England, with Tamworth as his headquarters. By ritual and with counsel, the church was increasingly to the fore politically, while, during this period, the Anglo-Saxon warrior aristocracy inclined more towards being a group of landowners, with rights to land given legal title. Landowners became, as part of their contract, responsible for public works, such as bridges and fortifications, with Offa's Dyke, the immense protective barrier, between central England and Wales, the most notable example.

The Mercian supremacy was short-lived. Dynastic disorder prevailed. At the beginning of the 9th century, Wessex, led by Egbert, annexed Kent, Essex, Surrey and Sussex, and seemed to be heading for some degree of predominance. But this political thrust too, was soon cut short. Meanwhile, there hovered on the eastern horizon a dark threat to an England very far from unified and decidedly enfeebled by internal warring.

The peril came from the Norse races, in part from the Norwegians, who sailed round the north of Scotland and tended to concentrate on Ireland, Scotland, Wales and Cornwall and the north west of the British Isles, and the Danes, who attacked the east and south of England and also some of the Frankish lands. Population growth in cold and mountainous areas where agriculture was arduous was typically the causation for this latest Barbarian assault. It was conducted by men who coupled great navigational skills with an abrasive fierceness. The term Viking covered both groupings; it was coined by those they attacked and basically means 'pirate'.

Already in trading contacts with their future victims, the Norse assaults began with desultory raids and then developed into a military operation of deliberate policy. *The Anglo-Saxon Chronicle* relates the increasing horror experienced by the Anglo-Saxons, who, whatever their internal fractiousness, had been free from external danger for two hundred years. The first raids were in 789; after 835 they were less sporadic and more forceful; then in 865, the Danish 'Great Army' landed in and occupied East Anglia and soon easily took Northumbria.

The Danes found Wessex a harder nut to crack, but in 871 a second Danish army landed by way of reinforcement. It was now that Alfred the Great (871-899) made his mark. Firstly, he bought off the Danes and gained five years of relief, during which the Danish invaders conquered Mercia. In 875/6 a somewhat reduced host of Danes again moved against Wessex, but, after initial checks, Alfred succeeded in defeating them at the battle of Edington in 878. A deal was struck with the Danish leader, Guthrum, assisted by the fact that he had been converted to Christianity and felt inclined to befriend Alfred. In effect, the lands beyond a line running from London to Chester were controlled by the Danes.

The legend of Alfred as the saviour of England has a more limited meaning in reality, and he was never sure of the allegiance of other

English kings, let alone enjoying any authority over the Norse-held stretches of England. For all that, by diplomatic shrewdness as well as military skill he sustained an English base of unlikely strength. He nursed the proud sentiments of Mercia as well as keeping the Danes at arm's length. He busily constructed a series of fortified strongholds, such as Winchester and Oxford, that guaranteed Wessex security from further internal assaults, and he developed a more effective army and navy. That he also contrived, under the stressful pressure of his age, to advance learning and educational activity adds enormously to his already worthy reputation.

For their part, the Danes arrived in huge numbers, bringing their own customs, agrarian as well as cultural, to what became known as the Danelaw. The profusion of the 'thorp' suffix – Scunthorpe, Cleethorpes – testifies to this widespread settlement. Even when England became unified, the distinctive Danish element survived. That was some time in coming. The next decades were years of confused fighting and bargaining but, on the foundation carefully built by Alfred, there were successes. Needless to say, there were divisions among the Norsemen as well. Gradually, the royal house of Wessex was widely accepted amongst the English as the dominant kingship, that is, as the prospective royal family of England.

The reign of Edgar (959-975) marks the end of this complicated phase and the fulfilment of Alfred's ambition. The kingdom was unified under one king, whose authority was widespread and deeply etched. Laws were promulgated and upheld, with the Witan, a formal council with considerable influence including on occasion the appointment of kings, permanently instituted. The shire system was confirmed in a pattern that would last until 1974, while the localism of the hundreds ('wapentakes' in the old Danelaw) and the 'tithings' (each comprised of ten mutually responsible households) completed a most elaborate structure of local government. The English church and monasteries, with St Dunstan one of several outstanding clerics, not only found new strength but played a vital role in the contemporary reform of European Christianity. The church and its leading lights added greatly to the lustre of the new English monarchy.

Stability was relatively short-lived. The Danish monarchy had grown exceptionally powerful, with Denmark and Norway under the one king, and with a highly proficient army at his beck and call. England, with its natural Danish interest, was an obvious target. During the fateful 990s, the play and counter-play of Viking raids and English payments in tribute became a debilitating pattern, for which the reign of Aethelred the Unready became, perhaps a little unfairly, notorious. But one short-term action of his – marriage with the Duke of Normandy's daughter in an attempt to consolidate a treaty preventing the Danes using Normandy as a base – had long-term consequences of a fatal nature.

Matters were not helped by English paranoia, including a half-hearted and ill-thought out plan to massacre those of Danish heritage, a foolish act that brought the Scandinavians in aggressive force to England.

During the first decade of the second millennium, fortunes ebbed and flowed, until, in 1016, Cnut (often modified to Canute, and one whose is recalled in place-names like Knutsford) became king. A scion of the Danish royal household, who had been heartily engaged in the fighting on English soil, he was welcomed as monarch by both Danish supporters and by many English nobles.

The tale of his ordering back the sea has been turned topsy-turvy by many modern pens, whereas in truth, he was sensibly demonstrating to his sycophantic courtiers the limitations of kingship. His wisdom was more practically exhibited by his endeavours to reinforce both the legal system and the complementary mechanism of the church. Unluckily for England, he was drawn into the web of Scandinavian politics, for, in 1019, just a year or two into his reign, he inherited the whole of the large Danish empire and became more remote from English affairs. Nonetheless, there was comparative calm and well-being until his death in 1035. Indeed, the 11th century was marked by the evolution of most effective governmental methods. The need to raise 'Danegeld', taxes first to pay off the Danish invaders and second for the upkeep of a mainly Danish standing army, had led to the construction of a first-class financial system. It is intriguing to muse over the possibility that, had Cnut lived longer or established a more secure heritage, England might have developed as an Anglo-Danish rather than an Anglo-Norman kingdom.

Despite its political problems the last century of pre-Norman England was prosperous. Population increased as did trade and by that token, urban trading centres or 'ports'. Agriculture became more productive.

The shire court and the shire-reeve, or sheriff, were notable additions to the bipartite process of central and local government, while the use of the royal writ, a simple but highly effective kingly order, usually mediated through the sheriff or bishop, was to prove a mighty instrument of monarchical power.

The kingdom that William the Conqueror was about to occupy was no feeble land, but one with a thriving economy and an elaborate bureaucracy. William was to find the governmental structure invaluable for his purposes, while the monumental Domesday Survey was wholly dependent on the Anglo-Saxon precedents of record keeping.

The reign of Edward the Confessor, marked by the dominion of Godwin's family, ended in 1066, and Godwin's son, Harold, the powerful Earl of Wessex, succeeded him. He was immediately challenged by two rivals. The first was Harold Hardrada of Norway, asserting his right in the wake of Cnut, who invaded Northumbria and occupied York, forcing Harold, already anxious about a Norman attack, to move hurriedly north. He defeated the Norwegian force in a gory contest at Stamford Bridge, not far from York. The Norman invasion, whilst delayed by poor weather, was still ill-timed from Harold's viewpoint. Having won one battle on 25 September, he was obliged to undertake a forced march to fight another on 14 October, William having landed at Pevensey a fortnight or so earlier. A day long struggle just outside Hastings ensued; Harold was killed and William prevailed.

The marriage of Aethelred into the Duke of Normandy's family, coupled with the alleged tale of Harold having conceded his right to the crown, gave William a legal case to support his conquest. The Normans, as their name suggests, were themselves of Norse origins. They had etched out a convenient enclave on Frankish soil, which became the base for what were to be among the last of the so-called Barbarian invasions. Just as their predecessors had colonised regions other than Britain, the Normans also occupied areas in Sicily and Southern Italy during the 1050s.

The Norman Conquest was very much an occupation rather than a settlement. William's 6000 strong army was largely a mercenary one, its professional archers and horsemen matched against the English peasant host, armed chiefly with battle axes and shields. Once the kingdom had been subdued, this army was soon demobilised. William the Conqueror brought with him a relatively small group of fellow nobles; there was no attempt to flood the country with Norman immigrants after the fashion of the Anglo- Danish settlements. It was an out-and-out military conquest.

Chapter 3
THE MIDDLE AGES FROM THE CONQUEST TO MAGNA CARTA
1066 – 1215

The consolidation of the Norman hegemony over England was, despite the dash and courage of Anglo-Saxon rebelliousness, fairly quickly complete. Utilising the English monarchical device of the King's writ to justify his military domination, William I contrived to do what no previous English king had quite managed. He enforced recognition of his title to all the land; the kingdom was his in the most literal sense. He then proceeded to parcel it out in usually large swathes to his immediate followers. For example, Roger of Poitou was granted all the land between the Mersey and the Ribble, the major portion of what would become Lancashire. In turn, he rewarded his senior subordinates with tenancies, and thus was the land subdivided, with reciprocal contracts of mutual obligation. If not always the classic Feudal System of the Frankish kingdom, it was a very practical representation of that principle.

Where the Romans had sought to assimilate the British into their culture and incorporate them as allies in the workings of government and defence or where the Anglo-Saxons and Danes had settled down as farmers over great parts of the country, bringing families and friends to join them, and with little reference to the previous occupants, the Normans were imperial colonists. The English populations of both high and low estate were subject to them, politically and economically. It has been estimated that in the decades following 1066 there were never more than 10,000 Normans, including their families, resident in England, holding in subjection a populace of something like 1.4m to 1.9m. It was a colonial pattern more like, say, the British Raj in India than the British development of Australia.

William remained Duke of Normandy. In other words, Normandy and England combined as a cross-Channel political entity. As Duke of Normandy, he owed some allegiance to the King of France, and so once more England was absorbed into continental politics and fashions. One needs to be reminded that water transport, especially with the neglect and decline of Roman roads, was the superior means of travel, so that the Franco-English link was easier than, for instance, a trip northwards from London by land.

It meant of course, that French was the language widely used, very much as an international language for governance and law. A picturesque sample of this effect is the usage of Anglo-Saxon terms for live domestic animals and Norman-French words for dead ones; hence cow/beef; chicken/poultry; calf/veal; pig/pork; deer/venison and sheep/mutton. Although disputed by some, it has been asserted that this arose from Anglo-Saxon underlings raising the live animals, then delivering them dead as rent in kind to their Norman-French overlords.

It is true that some Anglo-Saxons negotiated a deal with the Normans and welcomed them, but in essence, the native English lost much. At the time of the authoritative *Domesday Book* compilation in 1086, there were only two English landowners of any note. Four thousand English thegns, men of middling high rank holding moderately large portions of land, had been replaced by 200 Norman barons. In most areas up to 80% of the property was in Norman hands. William the Conqueror also made inroads into the church, well aware of its influential character. In 1070 he deposed several English bishops, substituted Norman ones and never appointed another English prelate.

The *Domesday Book* logged in detail the condition of England in 1086 in comparison with the situation appertaining before 1066. Some argue it is a massive tax register, a record of where all the wealth lay, so that taxes could be precisely assessed. Some claim it is a compelling political statement, a record of how predominant Norman control had become. Perhaps it was both. Most decisions in history have more than one motive.

Certainly Norman control was strict and ruthless. The Normans inherited the comprehensively effective local and regional government of their predecessors and utilised it busily. There was shift from a mainly oral convention to a much more bureaucratic parchment-orientated system. From the military standpoint, they built great stonework castles at strategic points. The two – the local government network and the fortress – were often coupled together. There may be a sheen of mythology about Robin Hood as the outlawed tormentor of the officious Normans, but there is a stern reality about the Shire-reeve, or Sheriff, of Nottingham lording it over the vicinity from the bowels of his impressive castle. The traditional moated castle with its drawbridge, keep and battlements became the abiding architectural symbol of the middle ages.

They were the emblem of a very real change of historical tempo. The coming and going of kings in the pre-Conquest era, even the coming and going of Roman governors in the pre-English period, had never dislocated the even tenor of land and property tenure on anything like the same scale. What the Norman Conquest did was to introduce wholesale into England a brand-new ruling elite as well as a new king.

It was around this version of kingship and a novel aristocracy that governance over the next two centuries and more was determined. The king's household was both central and powerful in this regard, often on the move, with huge costs to the localities visited. The Norman-French king's patronage was immense and it was lucrative, as scores of people jostled to be included in the wide-ranging service of the monarch. Naturally enough the hub of military command lay in the household and the term 'household cavalry' still echoes down the ages.

The presence of something akin to a national army rather than the more occasional 'feudal host' of yesteryear was matched by the definitive application of national justice. Particularly under the hand of Henry II, the number of royal judges conducting frequent assizes on a countrywide basis led to the adoption of a 'common law', replacing the system of local custom and usage. The Assize of Clarendon in 1166 and the Assize of Northampton in 1176 established a regular machinery for the trial by royal judges of serious crimes. Judges and lawyers grew more learned in their vocation, with jury trial coming more into focus.

The judicial system obviously brought some funds to assist monarchical government. The financing of government over these centuries rested on the king's authority, in particular, his overall control of land and patronage. Certainly until the 13th century, taxation as such, was a comparatively minor source of revenue, with land, fees from feudal lordship and judicial fines comprising nearly 90% of the total, which, round about mid-12th century would have been some £20,000 annually.

The church was another source of revenue and patronage – and it was a church overseen by strong papal authority growing steadily in strength. During the 12th century the diocesan and parochial structure still familiar today endured. The parochial apparatus of the church was underpinned by monasticism, a movement that continued to increase in density throughout the whole of Catholic Europe. During the period from the Conquest to the signing of the Magna Carta the number of religious houses sprang from 50 to 700, and the total of monks and nuns rose from 1000 to 13,000. Although the Benedictine houses remained by far the most numerous, there was now a wide variety of orders from which would-be entrants to the religious life might choose. Amid the difficulties of medieval existence, the tranquil if rigorous call of the contemplative life was perhaps understandable.

The manor – and the manorial system – is another of those characteristic tokens of medieval life. In the generations after the Norman Conquest the British economy stayed true to its nature as almost wholly agrarian. Probably as many as 93% of the population eked out their living from the land. The *Domesday Book* lists no less than 13,000 settlements, while it is a remarkable fact that four-fifths of the arable land farmed at the outbreak of the 1914-1918 War had been under the plough in 1066. Two-fifths of the population were 'villeins', and they had a substantial stake in tilling nearly half the land, whilst another more well-to-do eighth, known as 'sokemen' or 'freemen' farmed a fifth of the available soil. These peasants formed a distinct class, as opposed to a third of their countrymen who were the poorer 'cottars' or 'bordars', using just 5% of the land, that is, roughly speaking, a border around a cottage, with, beneath them, a tenth of the total, with no land at all.

The king and his tenants-in-chief, some 200 wealthy lay rentiers and 100 religious foundations held 75% of the wealth of the nation.

They granted some of their land to subtenants, usually knights, while their 'demesne' land, farmed for their own purposes, was often leased for money rents to middling farmers of the same social rank as the knights. Mainly for rent in kind, more occasionally as labourers, the English peasantry undertook the task of farming all this land. Town life remained restricted during this era, while what commerce there was continued to concentrate on woollen cloth, building, sea fishing, salt production, mining and metal-working. The silver penny was the standard and well-preserved coin, but this was predominantly a natural, as opposed to a money, economy.

Agricultural methods were little changed from Anglo-Saxon times. Yields barely increased. Before the 13th century, the two-field and the 'out' and 'in' field systems prevailed, the format dictated by the terrain, but ordinarily a simple matter of leaving one section fallow and ploughing the other year by year. Sowing and reaping by hand was time-consuming, while the reliance on animal dung for fertiliser was not only sporadic but expensive, as the stock had to be fed during the cold winter months.

It was therefore, a stagnating economy and it is likely that, by the date of Magna Carta in 1215, there had been little improvement in production for several hundred years. The school textbook reference to 'strip' farming has the fields divided into strips, so that the villeins or sokemen might have more or less fertile portions or shares nearer or further away from the water supply. It has long been argued that, for all its apparent fairness, this led to wasteful movement hither and yon of the workforce. While this may have been true, the words 'field' and 'strip' tend to be misleading as to size. The yields being so small, it took an enormous acreage of land to feed a relatively small population of 2m or so, with London, population 18,000 in 1086, the only town, by continental standards, of significance. This is where the contrast with 1914, when a population of 33m lived off the same acreage of land, with the help of imported goods, is so meaningful.

The 'strip', in many cases, would have been the size of a decent allotment or, say, half a football pitch, which certainly made the business of moving from one part to another something more arduous than teetering along a thin line between narrow ribbons of soil. Unhedged 'strips' arose from the need to keep the ploughed land free of encumbrance, for, after the harvest, it resorted to being the fallow ground.

In short, the lowly medieval villein required a substantial ration of land to ensure his family could be maintained above starvation level – and starvation and malnutrition was no uncommon feature of these times. The 13,000 named settlements of England were basically self-sufficient, with cash used very sparsely, and with the average population of such manorial hamlets no more than a hundred.

Thus, year on year over many decades, the large majority of the population worked hard in these tiny atomistic units to make ends meet, as the seasonal cycle of the agricultural wheel turned, the monotony broken only by the ministrations of the parish priest and the feast days associated with the Roman Catholic faith. It has been said that Roman Catholicism admirably suited the peasant existence, as it preached of a brief, harsh, earthly sojourn, spent in stolid acceptance of one's earthly plight, before the glory of heavenly salvation.

Not for them the high politics of the relatively small elite, who appeared to expend much time and energy on power squabbles. The medieval political history of England is closely interwoven with that of France.

Apart from disputes with the French, William I's successor sons, William Rufus and Henry I, had difficulties with their elder brother Robert who had become Duke of Normandy. The fissure between the two parts of the Anglo-Norman entity was a very dangerous one. The death of the able but troubled Henry I in 1135 then led to several years of disorder as his daughter Matilda and his nephew Stephen of Blois laboured one against the other for the succession.

The eventual breakthrough came in the form of Henry, the son of Geoffrey of Anjou, by then the ruler of Normandy, and Matilda. On his father's death, he inherited both Normandy and Anjou, where after, in 1150, he made a brilliant marriage with Eleanor of Aquitaine, weeks after her divorce from the French king Louis VII, thereby adding the rich territory of Aquitaine to his vast possessions. Henry Plantagenet, although faced with martial rivalry on all sides, fought on, and soon the barons in all areas, their estates weakened by incessant warfare, persuaded the antagonists to find a settlement. Stephen, especially after the death of his heir, Eustace, grew tired and disillusioned and agreed to hold the kingship for life and then be succeeded by Henry.

This was authenticated by the Treaty of Westminster in 1153 – and Henry died in 1154.

Henry II came to the throne and he reigned until 1189 as the first undisputed king for over a century, such was the inherent instability of the monarchy. Moreover, he ruled over a vast empire and was indisputably the most powerful ruler in Europe. He continued in like vein, restoring the border counties of England, which had fallen into Scottish hands, recovering the Norman Vexin, the area disputed with France, and occupying Britanny and other French regions. The trade between France and England – chiefly salt and wine for cloth – brought him fruitful revenues in customs and other taxes and, in general, his was a successful and highly efficient reign. Given the extent of his domains, it followed that the apparatus of local government had to be rationalised. Henry II is regarded as the king who consolidated the common law, an impressive achievement.

That said, the fact that he spent 21 years of his 34 year rule on the continent, reigning over the vast Angevin Empire, is a wry reminder that England per se was something of a backwater compared with culturally brighter and commercially sharper France, and yet another pointer to the continuing progress of British in the shadow of Western European history.

Henry II's most famous English exploit was his rift with his former Chancellor, Thomas Becket, when the king made that ambitious official Archbishop of Canterbury. The quarrel was founded in disputes over the clash of secular and ecclesiastical authority. William Rufus and Henry I had already had rancorous arguments with Anselm, Archbishop of Canterbury, over the primacy of power as between church and state. This raised posers everywhere in Christendom – for example, should 'criminous clerks' be tried in lay courts? – but they were often settled in conciliatory fashion. In the Constitution of Clarendon of 1164, Henry II requested the clergy to agree to observe his customary rights over the church, but Thomas Becket, having first agreed, then revoked his agreement. Charges were laid against him and his estates were made forfeit, leading him to go into a six year exile. His return, ostensibly to punish the clergy who had participated in the coronation of Prince Henry as Henry II's heir, was the next cause of the king's wrath and Becket's 'Murder in the Cathedral'. Catholic Europe was aghast; Becket was quickly canonised, but, in real terms, his death ended the confusion in the English church and stability was the pleasing outcome.

For nearly twenty more years this most creative of kings stayed at the height of his powers, but, inescapably, his last years were spoilt by rebellious sons, avid to grab their portion of the vast Angevin empire. Two sons – Henry and Geoffrey – died, whereat Richard, noting his father's partiality for John, collaborated with Philip Augustus II, the wily and belligerent king of France, to thwart him. This they contrived to do and on Henry II's death, Richard I became king in 1189. Almost immediately he left for the Crusade, where he proved a highly capable opponent for the great Saladin. Only eight months of his ten years reign were actually spent on English soil but he compensated for this by the appointment of Hubert Walter as justiciar, or chief minister, and as Archbishop of Canterbury. He was but one of a long line of sane and shrewd advisers who, over the years, brought composure and efficiency to English monarchical governance.

Richard's brother John succeeded him but his troubles, many of them self-made, soon confounded him. Unpopular taxation at a time of high inflation, squabbles with the church and the failure of his continental ventures were followed by baronial rebellion in England itself. The rebels captured London and John was forced, in 1215, to sign the document that became known as Magna Carta, primarily a statement of the baron's rights in the face of overmighty kingly authority. It was an insincere signature and the quarrel continued. Not long after the famous incident when he lost his baggage in the quicksands of the Wash, King John, admired by some modern historians but basically incapable of reining in his powerful magnates, died in 1216, leaving a country torn by civil strife.

During the period from the Conquest to Magna Carta, non-English Britain remained largely independent. Wales, despite the efforts of western based earls to make headway therein, managed by a combine of harsh terrain and spirited princes among its several kingdoms to stay free of English rule. Ireland too, although subject to some of the same venturesome enterprise of Norman earls, contrived to retain its autonomy, while Scotland, for the most part, stayed clear of too much involvement in the political and military entanglements that criss-crossed England and Western Europe. In an era of stability, the Scottish kings witnessed both expansion into the northern highlands and along the western seaboard and also urban and other development in the lowlands.

In the main, the century and a half from 1066 to the famed signing of Magna Carta may be summarised as one in which the ordinary folk went stolidly about their business of farming the land while their purported superiors indulged in extravagant and wounding political activities. Unless the latter happened to be located close to the former, everyday existence continued without much change.

Magna Carta acts as a dividing line more for its future use as a ringing symbol for English liberties than for its immediate implementation. Even so, the coming centuries were to bring, over against the prevailing medieval character of the era, some changes to both the Anglo-Saxon peasant farmer and their Norman-French overlords.

Chapter 4
THE LATER MEDIEVAL AGE
1216 – 1485

When King John's young son mounted the throne in 1216 there were 250 years to run of the medieval epoch, commonly regarded as terminating with the onset of the Tudor dynasty in 1485. In the main, the medieval nature of British existence persisted. The lower classes toiled away on the land, while their masters fought and wrangled over mainly familial disputes throughout the British Isles and across Western Europe. The low, slow temperature of the one was at acute contrast with the heated, rapidly moving tempo of the other.

First let us unravel the torturous skein of the feudal-cum-dynastic warfare of those centuries. Henry III (1216-1272), soon found troubles abounding at home and abroad. He was forced to forego almost all claims to French territory, whilst domestically the great magnates rose against him. In 1258/59 they proposed an aristocratic council – sometimes viewed as the precursor of Parliament – to oversee

England. The subsequent war ended in 1265 with the defeat of the council's leading light, Simon de Montfort.

Henry's son, Edward I (1272-1307) thus inherited a formally accepted monarchy and proceeded to attempt the subjugation of Wales and Scotland. By 1283, Wales, subdivided into petty kingdoms, was overcome and a formidable, if expensive, line of castles – Caernarfon, Harlech, Conwy and the rest – was built to subdue the Welsh. Seizing on a weakness in the succession to the Scottish throne, Edward initiated a lengthy period of enmity with the Scots. The vigorous response of chieftains like Robert Bruce and William Wallace, and the Scottish triumph at the Battle of Bannockburn in 1314, gave notice that the conquest of Scotland would be a wearisome business. Moreover, the monarchy's slim grasp on Ireland worsened and was both costly and perfunctory.

Between the deaths of Edward I in 1307 and of Richard III in 1485, no less than seven kings ruled England, and most of them were involved in excursions into Scotland or France. Edward II (1307-1327), a thoroughly inadequate ruler, was forced to abdicate in favour of his son, Edward III (1327-1377) a much more prepossessing figure. While retaining a firm grip on home affairs, he was extremely ambitious, and, on the basis of his mother being French, made bold to claim the French throne. He inaugurated in 1337 that set of desultory and inconclusive campaigns that scarcely merit the grandiose title of the Hundred Years War. There were some high spots. There were victories at the Battle of Crecy in 1346, plus the capture of Calais, and, through the chivalric efforts of his son, the Black Prince, at Poitiers in 1356, but the outcome was ever indeterminate and the process extremely burdensome.

Edward III's second son succeeded him as Richard II (1377-1399) but, self-willed and insecure, he found himself at odds with the senior aristocracy and Henry Bolingbroke, a grandson of Edward III, replaced him as Henry IV. The great magnates retained, even augmented, their authority and the dynastic rift to which the royal linage was prone reopened.

The crucial divide was between the Lancastrian grouping created around Henry IV's father, John of Gaunt (the richest magnate with an annual income of £12,000), and the Yorkist set that surrounded the claimant the Earl of March. Although relations with Scotland, were marginally improved, Ireland was less placable. Nonetheless, the independently-minded Anglo-Irish lords delivered security from foreign assault. It was Wales that was the Celtic bugbear in the 15th century. Neither the crown nor the Marcher lords, many of them allies of the Earl of March, could control the rebellious Welsh. Henry IV's reign was punctured with repulsing the Welsh uprisings led by Owain Glyndwr and with struggles against his aristocratic foes. For all this, he persevered and was able to hand over a reasonably stable state to his son, Henry V (1413-1423). Henry V provided the one shining page in an otherwise dark and wearisome tale.

Soon after suppressing a revolt on behalf of the Earl of March, the ambitious young king decided on an extensive and highly popular campaign in France, reviving old claims at a juncture when France was feebly governed. Henry V was, rather like several of his predecessors, to spend almost half his reign on the continent. The centrepiece was the Battle of Agincourt in 1415, when the feared potency of English archery enjoyed its finest medieval hour and the French were routed. Consequent successes in Normandy enabled Henry V to negotiate the favourable Treaty of Troyes in 1420 that made him regent to the ailing French king, Charles VI, and heir to the French crown.

It was the zenith of English authority in France. The premature death of Henry was however, a serious blow, and his baby son, Henry VI (1422-1461), hailed also as Henry II of France, was faced with untold difficulty. The resurgence of the French, inspired by Joan of Arc, rocked the English confidence and years of protracted warring and uneasy truces followed. In 1453 the Hundred Years War ended ignominiously. It was a heavy defeat for the English and a complete loss, except for Calais, of all of Henry V's amazing gains.

Within weeks Henry VI, well-intentioned but incapable, fell gravely ill and the Wars of the Roses were soon in full swing. A most messy phase of changing crowns, royal deaths, sporadic fighting and often unstable governance followed. At first the House of York with the competent Edward IV and the wily Richard III as monarchs held sway.

But hereditary monarchy continued to demonstrate its fickle nature. Richard III was himself toppled. The dynastic struggles – which, for all their significance had occupied only fifteen months of the last thirty years in actual fighting – ended in 1485 at the battle of Bosworth Field. Henry Tudor, destined to be Henry VII, had landed from France, trailing a somewhat tenuous claim based on his mother's descent from Edward III's son, John. That meant little compared with his positive win, coupled with the death in battle of Richard III, who had no direct heir. Yorkists and Lancastrians alike were weary of and impoverished by decades of strife and both sides were wooed by Henry VII, as he undertook the massive task of managing England's fortunes.

During the medieval period, that is, from 1066 to 1485, five of England's eighteen kings died outside England – a mark of the confused involvement of these islands with the continent throughout this time. Self-sufficient agriculture based on the manorial system remained the dominant economic characteristic. Medieval warfare was sporadic and, while destructive in the localities where waged, did not interfere unduly with the common round of farming, although there were troubles enough from famine, flooding and animal diseases. The resources and will of the baronial and other families directly involved were weakened. One consequence was a move by manorial lords, their resources wasted by war, to shake up the old-fashioned system of strip-field agriculture with attempts to create larger money-making farms.

Indeed, recurrent war acted as a catalyst as well as a destroyer. The military – think of all those archers at Agincourt – and increasingly, the navy, offered employment opportunities, while the sinews of war required supplies of all kinds, a stimulus to the nascent trading and manufacturing element in the economy. War was expensive but, a truism, the money that was raised to fight wars was also being spent.

In the main, England's commerce arose directly from land usage. Mining, such as Cornish tin and Newcastle coals, was relatively small scale; mercantile shipping, other than in coastal waters, was limited, while English bankers and merchants could scarcely compete with their wealthy continental equivalents. Pastoral farming, however, was now in the ascendant, with British wool much in demand. By the 14th century there were perhaps as many as 18m sheep, many of them large beasts, in the country, with some flocks, often managed by religious houses, numbering 10,000. At this stage, the average annual export of wool was 20,000 sacks, each sack carrying a minimum of 250 fleeces.

This slow switch to more commercial forms of economic life naturally led to increased town-life. In fact, this had, after a definite plateau in urban development since the Norman Conquest, occurred since the late 12th century, often with lords, hopeful of gain, planning new towns with a monetary edge, such as coastal ports, like Hull or King's Lynn. The general run of towns were founded on their market – there were well over a thousand markets and fairs at this point – but by and large, they provided only a localised custom coming from within a maximum of twenty miles radius. Ordinary life was still prescribed in very limited geographical terms.

Population obviously had an effect on the rise of the number of towns and the number of their residents. During the later medieval period, the demographic pressures were acute, but in opposing ways. In the first place, there was a sudden increase of population from about 3.5m at the time of Magna Carta to perhaps more than 4m in the 1320s. London was now a flourishing city of 45,000 inhabitants. The economic response to this likely trebling of the population was not positive. Agricultural habits, both of method and management, were still conservative.

Britain was, over against the food that could be provided, choked with people, and, especially as manorial lords sought to maximise their profits by more large-scale farming, the labour force began to suffer badly. By the 14th century, with prices high and land scarce, the peasantry found themselves faced not only with a wage rather than a subsistence existence, but with a wage lowered by an over-stocked labour market. While merchants and magnates thrived on high prices, a skilled carpenter found himself in receipt of 3d a day; an agricultural or other labourer just a solitary penny. A novel feature of later medievalism was the occasional outbreak of complaint, including rent-strikes and some violence, among a depressed work-force.

Population, having peaked, then dived abnormally. Starvation, malnourishment, illness and heightened mortality reaped a grim harvest. Then came the gravest natural disaster ever faced by the British people – the Black Death. Commonly thought to have been the bubonic plague, initially carried by infected rats, it entered by the southern ports in 1348 and by the end of 1349 it had spread to central Scotland as well as badly affecting Wales and Ireland. There were recurrences for a long time, particularly in 1360/62, 1369 and

1372. It was an ugly calamity that reduced the population by a third – down quite abruptly to not much more than 2m, back to something like the numbers at the time of the Norman Conquest.

It would be difficult to overrate the psychological as well as the physical damage of the catastrophe. Nonetheless, human resilience enabled the British people slowly to formulate a sort of recovery. It amounted to a strange compound of advantages and disadvantages, something akin to a turnover from those of the preceding era. The critical labour shortage offered some benefit to the previously exploited peasantry, for they could bargain for improved wages, while the landowners were faced with heavier costs and reduced markets at home and abroad. As ever, some prospered as others failed, with the French wars playing their role on this economic stage. Some well-placed gentlemen made money from their service to, for instance, Henry V in his spectacular victories, and rose in rank and wealth, whilst others foundered. Moreover, the French wars disrupted the Flemish cloth trade and – in another example of economic topsyturvydom – the English cloth industry flourished, aided by changes in English fashion. The Cotswolds, with Bristol enjoying further reinforcement as England's second city, East Anglia and Yorkshire were the chief centres. London too, continued to burgeon as the entrepot for North Sea, Baltic and Mediterranean markets; despite all the problems, it contrived to house as many as 50,000 citizens by 1500.

Internal war, plague and economic changes crucially affected settlement. There were lost villages and vacant estates, while the switch in the usage of wool brought, for instance, decay to wool ports like Boston and King's Lynn and growth to cloth towns like Bradford and Halifax.

There were undoubtedly strains, most notably demonstrated by the Peasants' Revolt of 1381, when disaffected agricultural workers from East Anglia and south-eastern England, allied with Londoners and other townsfolk, caused violent upheaval. The immediate complaint was the imposition of yet another poll tax, one of a series, this one costing a shilling a head. The broad appeal of the insurrection was caused by underlying political and even some religious dissension added to the economic dislocations, during which many landowners, including several large church holdings, had endeavoured to clutch on to feudal working reins outmoded by the more commercialised mood of the day.

Wat Tyler, the Kentish leader of the rising, and his followers, had progressive notions about the complete abolition of serfdom and the responsibilities of landholding, but its feeble organisation soon led to its overthrow. In 1450, during the reign of Henry VI, there was another among several such popular uprisings when John Cade and his supporters managed to gain a footing in London for a few days. None was successful, except in so far as they frightened the establishment, but the very idea of a popular insurrection – as opposed, of course, to an aristocratic one – had been practically unknown in England.

Wat Tyler's main accomplice was a demagogic cleric by the name of John Ball, a reminder that the medieval church as well as secular society had its mavericks, whilst his isolated failure reminds that Catholic Christianity endured as the all-consuming faith of the British Isles. The church was very much enriched from the 12th century by the tremendous growth of the religious orders. There were almost a thousand houses and nearly 20,000 members of a variety of religious orders in the early 14th century. The richness of this movement did have the drawbacks of being cloistered, thus removed somewhat from the ordinary populace, and with its vested interests protected by the strength of papal jurisdiction and canon law. This was a common issue across Christendom and one solution was the rise of the mendicant orders, international in format, cutting straight through the monastic and diocesan lines of organisation and interest, dynamic where the other was static, and adding colourfully and energetically to the pastoral care of the people. Beginning with the Dominicans in 1223 and the Franciscans in 1224, the friars had 350 houses in Britain by the end of the century.

Despite the continuing influence of Catholicism, there were increased signs, as in other countries, of a distinctive national character. The English suspected the French control of the later medieval papacy, an authority over which they have usually lacked influence. It is worth recalling that there has been only one English-born Pope, Nicholas Breakspear, for just five years in the 1150s. No Pope ever visited Britain until 1982. In practice, both monarchy and magnates were interlocked with the church in many social and economic ways. The church was a great landowner; churchmen were often key state administrators; the king and nobility were fruitful patrons of the church; papal jurisdiction giving 'benefit of clergy' was severely undermined by English law; papal taxation was seriously restricted and frequently channelled into the king's coffers, and papal appointments to senior posts were almost non-existent.

The clergy from bishops to priests, usually colluded happily with this process, one reason being that the secular authorities were just as worried about heresy, fearing its insurrectionary tendencies, as was the church. The only compelling heretical movement during the medieval age was Lollardy. The Lollards (supposedly from a word meaning mumbler, that is, of prayers) were inspired by the Oxford intellectual, John Wycliffe, a critic of unworthy, over-rich clergy. The Lollards wrote polemically in English and were responsible for the first English translation of the bible in 1396, but they dwindled to an isolated sect. Orthodoxy, especially in the mind of a strict king like Henry IV, the monarch who added burning to the punishments for heresy, ruled majestically.

In one sense, the Lollards' usage of English marked a general increase in literacy and a wider deployment of English in society. By the late 14th and into the 15th centuries, literacy outside the clergy and among several crafts and trades was much more commonplace. Sir Thomas More claimed, perhaps a little over-enthusiastically, that by the end of the 15th century, 50% of Englishmen, not, it should be noted, Englishwomen, were literate.

The more general use of English for written purposes, and by that token, the decline of French and Latin, was marked. Parliamentary affairs were discussed and recorded in English from mid-14th century. Linguistic history is most significant. The feudalistic divisions of old Britain had very distinct regional dialects and, in the case of the Celtic folk-groups, languages. Geoffrey Chaucer bemoaned the fact that his publications could not be understood across the land. During the 15th century, with the more extensive use of written English for official communications, there grew a widening acceptance of a received English tongue. With a geographically neat coincidence, the midland patois emerged as more or less the standard usage. The undisputed character of London as the capital city, where, through the recent substantial migration thence of many midlanders and easterners, that dialect had been firmly established, was a leading reason for this.

Forthwith both written and spoken English abided by this model – and there was a veritable outpouring of English prose and poetry. Chaucer, whose luxuriously panoramic study, *The Canterbury Tales* (1386-1400) is the undoubted masterpiece of this blossoming era, well merits his title as 'the father of English Literature'.

The political aspect attendant upon the nascent Anglicisation of the country, as indicated by religion, language and also architecture – witness the soaring perpendicular line of King's College, Cambridge – was the growing centralisation of government, a major feature of which was, without doubt, the end of the Hundred Years' War and the acceptance that the Anglo-French duality was at an end. In politics, as with language, England was a compact realm, unbothered by foreign claims and likelier to pursue proper territorial control of Wales, Scotland and Ireland. On the other side of the coin, and especially as the Wars of the Roses took their toll, the old-style feudal divisions became less well-defined and the feudal lords less powerful.

The English king was a powerful figure, holding the keys to genuine mastery of the kingdom, along with untold patronage and an aura of unparalleled majesty. Ironically, one cause of the tumult that characterised medieval monarchy was the size of the glittering prize – it attracted many competitors. Across the nation the sheriffs and the newly created justices of the peace did his bidding, while, crucially, the role of Parliament became consolidated. The commons, the local representatives of the laity, became more assured in their standing, as Parliament – 'the community of the realm' – took some control, as the king's instrument, of taxation, judicial review and law-making. The monarchy was becoming much more aware of the necessity to unite the country behind the actions that it took, whether support for war or changes of laws, and was also becoming more careful of its lines of communications with the realm.

Parliament met frequently, an average of once a year between 1327 and 1437 – and eventually it met exclusively at Westminster. With Westminster Abbey the spiritual locus of the monarchy and with government offices becoming settled there and in the City, London became much more the real governing capital of the nation. It had been the habit for the king to travel with his court, and for parliaments to be held wherever he was. When Edward III had tried to rule from abroad there had been irate protests, with a grave political crisis resulting, 1339 to 1343. This led sensible kings, like Henry V, to establish the apparatus of governance securely in the capital city. London was the political, as well as the economic, centre of a burgeoning nation.

Unlike the abrupt rupture of the Norman Conquest, very much like the much more gradual switch from Romano-British to Anglo-Saxon England, these significant alterations were slow moving. The medieval character of competing dynasties, often carrying their rivalries across the Channel, with an enduring structure of manorial farming the lot of the majority, had not yet quite changed. However, there were shifts towards a larger money economy and extended commercial sector, towards a more Anglicised religiosity, towards a greater national sensibility, notably in language and culture, towards a constitution in which Parliament played a more influential role and towards a centralised monarchy and administration based on London. All these were harbingers, now observable with hindsight, of a country struggling towards a genuine nationhood. Under the Tudors the transformation from feudal kingdom to absolute nation-state would be rapidly progressed.

Chapter 5
THE MAKING OF A NATION
(1485-1742)

The quarter of a millennium that elapsed between the accession of Henry VII in 1485 and the fall of Robert Walpole as first minister in 1742 forms a momentous epoch in the British story.

Those very names betoken some of that significance; by the later date the collapse of a commoner, albeit a powerful one, was perhaps more important than the advent of a king. By the 18th century a constitutional monarchy had been firmly constructed – one in which sovereignty was vested in the King in Parliament, with Parliament, legally and practically, very much the seat of authority. The puissant Tudor monarchs oversaw the creation of a nation-state, centralised and compact, out of the previous rather messy feudal polity, riven by feuding at home and confused by interrelationships with the continent. They did so by exercising greater power than the feudal kings had dared, but during the 17th century their absolute power was gradually diluted as parliament gained in strength, so much so that by the 18th century we are able to speak of Sir Robert Walpole as Britain's first prime minister, effectively the ruler of the country.

All this occurred against a canvas of compelling geographic, technical and commercial change, with a substantive gloss of cultural and religious pigmentation. Although the oriental travels of the likes of Vasco da Gama and Marco Polo had excited European traders and others, it was just seven years after the ascent to the throne of Henry VII, when, in 1492, Christopher Columbus discovered – or, in justice to our fellow-humans living there, opened western eyes to the promise of – the new world. English explorers, like Sir Walter Raleigh, founder of the Virginian settlement, or Sir Francis Drake, the first Englishman to circumnavigate the globe, soon sailed westwards while later in this period, events such of the sailing of the Pilgrim Fathers in 1620 on the *Mayflower* to the eastern seaboard of America or the development of the West Indian colonies, ensured a British foothold on the vast new continent.

Of a sudden, Britain was transformed from being a relatively peripheral area on the edge of the known European world to being the central focus of a global planet. It changed not just how the British thought about Britain but how everyone else thought about Britain.

The stability brought by the Tudors was a priceless asset throughout the 16th century. These were often dark and turbulent times but the monarchy endured stalwartly. Henry VII, Henry VIII and the imperious Elizabeth I clocked up 109 years of unimpeded ruling, with just the short reigns of Edward VI and Mary I, barely eleven years in sum, by way of stark contrast. It was a simple three-generational model of Henry VII, his son and his three grand-children. There were occasional challenges; the tragic episode in 1553 of the fated Lady Jane Gray in dispute with Queen Mary or the danger posed to Elizabeth by her cousin, Mary Queen of Scots, who was executed in 1587, are examples – the ruthless disposal of both pretenders characterises how lacking in bite were these claims, compared with the enfeebling dynastic struggles of medieval times. There were some internal troubles, such as the Pilgrimage of Grace in 1536 and the Northern Rebellion of 1569, both of them with a religious bias, but these uprisings and others were cruelly and rapidly crushed.

Something of the same is true about war. Although Tudor kings bore in mind the French question and, for instance, Henry VII, Henry VIII and Mary were all involved in minor if expensive wars with France, they were not as exacting as their medieval equivalents. The most threatening risk was posed by hostilities with Spain – motivated by a mix of religious antagonism, for Spain remained strictly Roman Catholic as England, like much of non-Latin Europe, opted for Protestantism – and rivalry over the wealth to be sought in the new world. The Spanish empire in South America had become England's sternest trading competitor. The sailing of the Spanish Armada in 1588 and its subsequent out-manoeuvring by the English fleet and dispersal by tempestuous weather, was the closest that Britain itself came to actual invasion during this period.

As such illustrations remind, the political events of the age were driven more by diplomatic, mercantile and theological reasons than by family quests for title over continental pickings. It all pointed to kingdoms beginning to metamorphose into nation-states, described by the historian of civilisations Arnold Toynbee as 'the pagan deification' of slabs of territory. The religious enmity that led to early modern wars was caused by the rise of Protestantism, its origins usually dated from Martin Luther's Wittenberg theses of 1517. Critical although the theological divisions were – as one side held to the view that the priest and the sacraments were the only avenue to salvation, while the other argued for the primacy of the individual and the weight of the scriptures – of more immediate political significance was the role of religion as a control mechanism.

English Protestantism, in initial effect, was ecclesiastical, not theological. Henry's first wife, Catherine of Aragon, had during their long marriage produced but one child and that a daughter, later to be Mary I (1553-58), and the king was keen for a divorce and a wedding with Anne Boleyn, mother of Elizabeth I (1558-1603). To complete the trio of royals, when Anne Boleyn fell foul of Henry, it was his third wife, Jane Seymour, who provided his only son, the learned but shortlived Edward VI (1547-53). The church was taken over by the state, in the name of Henry VIII, in the 1530s with, at first, negligible alteration to its ceremonies and rituals. Amid a flurry of legislation, the Act of Appeals, 1533, and the Act of Supremacy, 1534, were two of the chief statutes. The new Church of England was enabled to do the monarch's bidding, grant his divorce and set the stage for English Protestantism.

The Dissolution of the Monasteries followed. Henry VIII was wary of the extra-national links of these foundations and fearful that they would remain bastions of papal authority. He was also eager to tap into their vast wealth, while, in truth, there were sufficient nasty examples of backsliding in the monasteries to justify stern reform. The *Valor Ecclesiasticus*, the first major tax survey since the *Domesday Book*, was undertaken with superb precision and expedition, leading to the sale of monastic lands to the nobility and gentry, fulfilling the twin aims of raising much-needed – and quickly spent – revenue for the crown and tying in the upper and middle ranks of the laity to the novel religious settlement. The monasteries had owned close on a fifth of English manors; now this was reduced to a small percentage, whilst the gentry had lifted their share of manors from three-fifths to three-quarters.

The administrative genius responsible for both the essential parliamentary legislation and the sale of the monasteries was Thomas Cromwell, a protégé of Cardinal Wolsey, Henry VIII's first and disgraced Chancellor and successor as first minister to Thomas More, a fervent protagonist of the papal position. An understated historical figure, perhaps because he was mainly a backstage operator, he is believed by many commentators to be the constructor of the centralised state apparatus that was the political dimension of the nascent nation-state. Parliament worked with the crown as the fount of sovereignty, creating an omnicompetent national government for the first time, while the unwieldy Council of the hard-working and prudent Henry VII became the Privy Council, an executive body of some nineteen members, almost akin to a cabinet of later times. It devised and enforced policy, oversaw the law courts, supervised government finances and, through the justices of the peace and other lay representatives, controlled much of local government. The partnership of crown and gentry was complete. This was to be called the Tudor 'revolution in government' and, all in all, the 1530s emerged with a claim on being the most significant decade in the construction of the British state.

Importantly, that same phase showed a remarkable spring in population, long stagnant since the years of the Black Death. The English population was static at 2.75m in 1535, but by 1603 it had increased to 4.10m. This had major implications. Heightened demand was a chief factor in what the famous economic historian, R.H.Tawney, was to term the '16th century Agrarian Revolution', a wholesale commercialisation of agriculture, with conjoined common and waste lands subject to 'enclosures' and the emergence of large and profitable farms. Vagrancy and unemployment was the severe downside, while there was also a Price Revolution, the consequence of cheap labour, imports of gold from the new world, heavy government spending and debasement of the coinage. In an extremely brief precis of an extremely complex issue, food prices rose very steeply and the real value of wages fell to very low levels over the Tudor period.

Yet, despite the price paid by the weaker and more vulnerable of the populace, the mood was optimistic as, overall, the newly-formed nation-state evolved in parallel with a newly-formed money-economy leaving behind all but a few vestiges of the old natural economy. As part of that there emerged a forceful class of 'gentry', commercially-minded farmers and merchants highly supportive of the stability and opportunities afforded by a strong and generally peaceable state. Urban development, flavoured by the characteristic Tudor architecture and with, patently, London the dominant and flourishing leader, moved on apace.

The 16th century, bountiful in its revolutions, was also witness to the Scientific Revolution, like the Reformation a cross-European phenomenon, whereby a much more rational, secular and evidence-based attitude was adopted to the material world. The philosopher Francis Bacon, who died in 1626, was a vigorous proponent of the cause – eager 'to win a victory over nature' – while in the coming 17th century, men like Isaac Newton or William Harvey, describer of the circulation of blood, would sustain that more scientific approach. This deeper understanding of the physical dimension, building on earlier discoveries, had an immense practical application, with novel navigational instruments, such as the magnetic compass, first used sometime after 1300, of much value in sea-bound exploration. Gunpowder, first utilised in Europe in 1320 for military purposes, is another obvious example of technical change; few medieval castles, for instance, could withstand the cannon – and the face of war was modernised.

In so far as one other 'revolution' – the Renaissance – affected Britain, a further device, that of printing, with William Caxton setting up his first press in 1476, was to have unfathomable ramifications, not least in the consolidation of the received English language. Literature and drama was, of course, the main contribution of the English to the notion of a less church dominated arts arena, with the immortal William Shakespeare perhaps Britain's most renowned citizen ever. The distinction between *Hamlet*, secular, humanist and individualistic, and the best known medieval morality play, *Everyman*, religious, universal and anonymous, is an apt summation of the cultural switch from medievalism to modernism. It was as if a vertical slice had been carved from the horizontal shape of Latinate Christendom; it was self-consciously and self-evidently an English state, with an absolute monarchy and with the other parts of the British Isles its satellites.

This tumultuous and revolutionary era is probably the most significant century of British history. It is the perfect illustration of the historian's favourite shorthand word of 'interaction'. Each dimension of human life stimulated and was stimulated by the others, creating a complicated skein of basic change. For instance, the economic and social shift to a thriving money economy boosted and was boosted by scientific and technical enquiry; it supplied the revenue and local support for the new political system and was, in turn, encouraged and protected by the state; it was fuelled by the proceeds of former Roman Catholic funds and found the more bible-based and individualist Protestant creed conducive to commercial and business practice, and in lieu of the church, it patronised literature, theatre and the arts, while reciprocally finding much sustenance in the advent of national sentiment and language.

The consequent Stuart age, roughly occupying the 17th century, was a boisterous epoch, frequently violent and highly coloured. That said, the changes were less fundamental than the previous era, except in one regard. The business of exploration and migration continued, including the momentous foundation of the American colonies, and by and large the financial and trading arms of the nation stayed strong, even stronger, in spite of the often difficult conditions, while contentions with European powers, including the Dutch as well as the French, were not uncommon.

Domestically, it was if the 1605 pro-Catholic gunpowder plot set the tone, with other more physical disasters, like the Great Fire of London in 1665 and the Plague visitation a year later, to follow. After the relative quietude of the reign of James I, the rule of his son, Charles I, was disrupted by the English and Scottish conflicts, plus harsh Irish campaigns, collectively the Civil Wars of the 1640s, the king's execution in 1649, the republican interregnum, with varied parliamentary and other expedients, with Oliver Cromwell, eventually the Lord Protector, the authoritative and towering figure.

The junior classroom oversimplification of sourpuss Roundheads versus wayward Cavaliers is, against the wider canvas, unhelpful. This was chiefly a complicated political puzzle. Oliver Cromwell – the only commoner to be head of state in over 2000 years of history – makes for a dramatic tale. Moreover, he managed, between the rather dingy and frivolous reigns respectively of the two Charles, to promote a stable, fruitful and respected regime. That social controls were severe possibly owes as much to fears of lawlessness in uneasy times as to puritanical piety. Cromwell restored some necessary equipoise to a riven nation and secured the base for a settlement, but he was a reluctant republican ruling over an uncomfortably kingless people.

The 1660 Restoration brought the unambitious Charles II to the throne, but his successor, Charles I's younger son, James II, was summarily deposed in the Glorious Revolution of 1688/89, ostensibly for harbouring Roman Catholic sympathies. This was just four years after his accession in 1685, at which time he had thwarted the Protestant pretender, Charles II's illegitimate son, the Duke of Monmouth, at the Battle of Sedgemoor and its gory aftermath. Now Dutch soldiers stood sentry on London streets as, in that bloodless coup, the champion of European Protestantism, William of Orange, son of James II's sister, shared the crown with his wife, Mary II, daughter of James II.

The one basic change to British political life after all this mayhem was the switch from an absolute to a constitutional form of monarchy. In effect, the process began in the unassuming year of 1641. The custom had evolved of monarchs calling Parliaments to agree taxation demands in return for 'redress of grievances', with the monarchs endeavouring to right social and economic wrongs as a quid pro quo of revenue for the governance of the country. Charles I, devious and indecisive in his political dealings, but an unyielding believer in the 'divine right of kings', was forced to cede many powers to an intransigent and active Parliament, one whose members were said to have been better versed in political knowledge than any other before or since. Control of the army, of religious matters, of choice of ministers, of financial affairs and critically, of the calling of Parliaments fell the way of Parliament. In truth, the former partnership, whereby king and Parliament had needed one another roughly equally had altered; the king found he needed Parliament more than it needed him. That there were high religious feelings, with the king wavering on the brink of Roman Catholicism whereas many Parliamentarians edged towards a more Puritanical view of worship, a prelude to the outbreak of English nonconformity, did not help.

It was as if new wine had been poured into new bottles. The system could barely cope with the novelty of the changes and the results were the explosive wars and contests of the 1640s and 1650s. The compromise agreement of the 1660 Restoration was further radicalised by the Glorious Revolution, and the accord of 1688/89 was not unlike the political condition of early 1642, by which time Parliament had taken a firm hand with the monarchy. Although kings and queens never lost all their powers and were often seen to be influential in foreign and political affairs, sovereignty after 1689 lay firmly with Parliament as the key maker of laws and other decisions. The reigns of Queen Anne, sister of Mary II, and of the four Georges, of the House of Hanover who followed her, were marked by the dominance of Parliamentary leaders and the beginnings of more formal Parliamentary factions or parties. Crucially, the king's first minister from 1721 to 1742 was Sir Robert Walpole, whose acute understanding of political situations and economic processes, enabled him to become not only the first but also the longest serving of what came to be termed prime ministers.

From mid-16th to mid-18th century the economic fabric of the nation flourished, with, from Oliver Cromwell to Robert Walpole, politicians eager to strengthen trade and the essential financial services to support it. Population began to pick up in numbers; it was 5.8m by the 1740s. The Bank of England, for example, was founded in 1694, while mercantile activity in the West Indies and increasingly

North America reaped princely gains. British arms were restored to some of their former greatness, with John Churchill, Duke of Marlborough's exploits at the Battle of Blenheim in 1704 and elsewhere at the expense of the French particularly noteworthy and valuable in the consolidation of British interests. And British was an adjective more readily deployed. In 1536, during the Tudor period, Wales had at long last been brought under the comprehensive rule of England and gradually all English laws and administrative customs were applied to the Principality, whilst Ireland, if often uneasily, remained under English hegemony. England and Scotland shared crowns from 1603 to 1707, when union was affected – from henceforward it was correct for Jane Austen to describe the British Isles very precisely as the United Kingdoms.

The Stuart Jacobites attempted to restore their monarchical fortunes in the risings of 1715 and 1745, but these were abject failures, with Bonnie Prince Charlie's following destroyed at the Battle of Culloden in 1746. Such colourful ventures are evidence that, despite the overall advance of the British state and its economy during the late 17th and early 18th centuries, there was an uneven tenor to the passage of history. The South Sea Bubble of 1721, a financial collapse of epic proportions for the times, is further evidence of socio-economic unease. It was an age of extravagance, waste and unruly disorder. One wit described the Hanoverian settlement as 'oligarchy moderated by riot'.

For all that, there was in hindsight, some kind of platform being erected upon which, in the last decades of the 18th century and throughout the 19th century, Britain would stage its proudest claim to be a top-class world power. One of the reasons for this would be that, during the Tudor and Stuart reigns, England had constructed a modern nation-state and developed the embryo of a parliamentary constitution, alongside the makings of a fruitful commercial economy and sound financial system. Other kingdoms had yet to face the traumas of revolutionary protest, economic change and incipient nationhood. The auguries were good for Britain.

Chapter 6
THE RISE AND FALL OF THE BRITISH EMPIRE
1742 – 2012

History tends to magnify the closer it approaches the present. An essay on almost half a millennium of Romano-British occupation may seem tenable. A similar attempt to record the British story over the last 270 years appears to be a much more awkward assignment, for their proximity makes the annals intense, familiar and immediate. There seems to be so much that dare not be omitted.

In examining the previous quarter millennium it was possible to find a mainline narrative, namely the creation of the English nation-state and its subsequent moderation from an absolute to a constitutional monarchy. Is it accomplishable to find such a strong thread for the remaining two and a half centuries of British history? Probably the nearest to a major plot-line is the ascent of Great Britain as the first and most puissant industrial power, controller of the largest Empire ever known to history, and arguably the world's most important nation, and its corresponding descent from that peak to a place in the global pecking order of middling not high rank, rather like that enjoyed by England in pre-Tudor times. This final narrative, then, describes the soaring rise and rapid fall of Britain and its Empire.

It is an epic tale that has its beginnings in the last decades of the 18th century, when British trade followed the flag in earnest, particularly under the ebullient leadership of the William Pitt the Elder, and when British arms were foremost in valour. Over against the later loss of the American colonies in 1783, English successes in the Seven Years War – Robert Clive's victory at the Battle of Plassey in 1757 and James Wolfe's capture of Quebec in 1759 – denied the combative French control of both India and North America. Later the courageous exploits of Lord Nelson (at Trafalgar in 1805) and the Duke of Wellington (especially against Napoleon at Waterloo in 1815) concluded the contest with the French, already weakened internally by the strife of the 1789 French Revolution and its aftermath. Most importantly, and apart from some relatively minor and mainly colonial hostilities, it would be a hundred years before Britain again had to fight a major European war, while, as opposed to its competitors, Britain's internal harmony was substantially more comfortable. Such an unprecedented epoch of domestic and overseas stability was to be a significant factor.

The reason for this zooming of British influence to its zenith was the interaction of three components; population, industrialism, and urbanisation. This interaction was vital but complex, almost a case of three chickens and three eggs, but the consequence was a mighty industrial nation of teeming town-dwellers.

In the 1740s the British population was a barely 6m, only two or three times its size in 1066. By the 1870s, in something more than a century, it had leapt to a flourishing 32m, a more than five-fold rise. Today it has doubled to over 60m. It was truly a demographic revolution. The numerical key was the decline in the death-rate, which fell by a half between the 1740s and the 1870s to 22 deaths per 1000 population, while the birth-rate remained constant at about 36 births per 1000 population. This produced a very youthful demographic, whereby the mean age, that at which half the population were either above or below, was 26; it is 40 at the present time. It is worth noting that the world at large followed suit in enduring a population explosion and on the same arithmetical pattern. It was about the same time that the British population had reached 30m that the global populace first touched 1bn; by 2025 it will be 8bn. Approaching 10% of the humans ever born are alive now.

Town-life became the norm. In the first half of the 19th century London's inhabitants doubled in number to 2m; Manchester and Salford jumped astronomically from less than 100,000 to 500,000; Leeds from 72,000 to 172,000 and Blackburn from 13,000 to 65,000. Bradford's population sprang eight times in number from 13,000 to 104,000. Town numbers grew at a faster rate than national numbers. Each decade about 0.5m people migrated from country to town. In 1701 Lancashire, destined to be the locus of industrialism, had but 101,000 inhabitants, By 1801 this figure was 673,000. By 1831 it was 1.4m. 10% of Britons now lived in Lancashire, most of them in its many growing towns; in 1701 it had been 0.5%. There were 1000 people for every square Lancastrian mile. When Queen Victoria came to the throne in 1837, the majority of British people lived in rural areas; when she died in 1901, by far the majority lived in urban areas, that is, in settlements of more than 5000 residents. By the end of the 20th century over 90% of the population lived in urban environs, covering some 10% of the actual land area.

Industrialisation was the third ingredient in the novel social mix. The 'Cottonopolis' of Manchester was 'the shock city of the 1840s', the world's first industrial city. In the 1780s there were two water-driven cotton mills in Manchester, and then the first steam-powered mill, courtesy of the revelation of the potency of steam by James Watt, was introduced in 1789. By 1800 there were 500 power looms in the country, with Manchester boasting 52 steam-driven cotton mills and 61 attendant iron foundries and machine shops. By 1833 there were 100,000 power looms in Lancashire alone and Manchester housed 213 mills and a vast array of other supportive industrial premises. The mill was the model for the factory system and, by 1850, the average number of workers per employment unit was 200. Hitherto work had been a much more solitary affair or conducted in penny numbers. Now five out of ten British manual workers were occupied in the industrial trades, the majority of them in large units such as steel or iron foundries, engineering or shipbuilding works and mines.

Together these enormous changes created the phenomenon which the political scientist, Herman Finer, laconically termed 'congregation'. More and more people pressed into the cabined conditions of more and more factory-type workplaces within the cramped confines of more and more crowded towns.

The railway was the crowning glory of the Industrial Revolution. Canals and improved roads had started the change in transportation, but the railway created an unprecedented transit network for both freight and passengers. Beginning with the Liverpool to Manchester link in 1830, there were 24,000 miles of rail in use by the end of the 19th century, with 1800m passenger journeys annually. Flying coaches and Macadamised roads had certainly reduced the London to Manchester journey from three days to one day, but the train managed it in a few short hours. It was a seismic shift in human experience. The nation was mobilised almost overnight. Then from 1819 transatlantic crossings by steamboat indicated that shipping was undergoing the same degree of industrialisation.

On this platform of steam power, Britain soared ahead as the original industrial power. There is little need to rehearse how, on the power front, gas, electricity, oil and nuclear energy came to play a pertinent role or how, in transportation, motorised and air travel supplemented and often superseded rail. Technology developed exponentially, with the bewildering electronics of the current age the latest example of scientific genius.

Domestically, industrialism brought in its wake social problems of dreadful character. Alongside the new urban conglomerations, there was often mass poverty and chronic epidemics of diseases like typhus and cholera. Gradually, as economic conditions improved, successive waves of endeavour by both central and local government introduced salutary measures, such as water supply, sanitation, gas and electricity, policing, schools, hospitals and other public provision. This mixture of a capitalistic economy with collectivist legislation of this kind culminated in the 'silent revolution' of Clement Attlee's Labour government, following the end of World War II, when all was consolidated into the Welfare State, with cradle to grave protection for all citizens, and with the National Health Service as the arch-stone of the edifice. Despite certain political ups and downs, this balance of a private enterprise economy with a social democratic collectivist system has endured to the present day.

Politically, and while the constitutional monarchy and parliamentary sovereignty remained in being, the leading story was of the extension of what had hitherto been a very limited franchise. Beginning with the seminal Parliamentary Reform Act of 1832 and ending with the Universal Suffrage Act of 1928, when both men and women over 21 were enfranchised, it was a lengthy process. It was paralleled by a sophistication of the political party system, the power base for such dominant statesmen as Sir Robert Peel, Benjamin Disraeli and Lord Salisbury, the chief Conservative leaders of the Victorian era, or William Gladstone, the long-lived and highly gifted Liberal giant, and his ebullient successor, David Lloyd-George. The clash of Conservative and Liberal politics remained the focus of the political struggle, until, during the 20th century, the Labour Party superseded the Liberals as the main left-leaning group.

Culturally, the Victorian age furnished glittering writers and artists in seeming accordance with the confidence and buoyancy of the times.

There was something of an integrated culture, a sharing of activities and thought among the earnest middle classes in alliance with the aspiring artisan classes. The novels of Charles Dickens and his worthy contemporaries, the comic operas of Gilbert and Sullivan, the enjoyment of the new-fangled seaside resorts and the spectatorship at cricket and football matches are examples, all against a backcloth of fairly puritanical religiosity. It is perhaps no coincidence that the three most influential thinkers of the modern epoch had British connections; Charles Darwin who was English born and bred; Karl Marx who spent the crucial part of his working life in London and Sigmund Freud, who, late in life, came to England as a refugee from German tyranny.

From a world perspective, of course, it was the British Empire, predicated on the effusion of industrial and fiscal power at home, that caught the historical eye. The steamship, as well as a strong navy and army, was the key both to expanding trade and colonisation, In 1860 the tonnage carried under sail outnumbered that conveyed by steam in the ratio of five to one; by 1910, that had been reversed to eight to one in favour of steam. During the Victorian period, the UK built two-thirds of all ships launched, with the British mercantile marine four times the size of Germany's, its nearest rival. In the forty years before World War I, British shipping earnings doubled from £38m to £76m. Jules Verne's *Round the World in Eighty Days* was not so much sci-fi as a classy advert. It was published in 1873 and in 1880 a ninety day round world trip was on offer for £200.

By dint of fighting and trading and treaty-making and administering, the British Empire, by 1900, covered 25% of the world's land surface, upon which resided no less than 700m souls, many of them of British stock, comprising a quarter of the world's population. Where the British stock far outweighed the indigenous people, as in Canada or in Australia, a quasi-independent 'dominion' status was granted; elsewhere colonial rule was conventionally autocratic. Sometimes there was undue harshness, but, in an era when the entire world was subject to degrees of what has been called 'Europeanisation', the British were by no means the worst of the colonial offenders. One fact is for sure. There can be no doubt that, for the only time in its history, Great Britain was the undisputed foremost nation of the world and the master of a bustling empire.

It was, in historical time, a short-lived triumph. Competitors hurried to emulate Britain in races that encompassed industrial development, overseas trade, colonial occupation and military and naval zeal, and behind the diplomatic complexities and dynastic entanglements of the day, this rivalry was probably the main factor in the descent into vicious warfare that characterised much of the 20th century. From the British perspective it was the converse of the relatively war-free 19th century. The 1914-1918 war, initially named the Great War, came as a shock to the national psyche and the industrial conversion of war from the set-piece battle to the lethal attrition of the trenches, with an unfathomable blood-letting, numbed all the combatant nations. A generation was decimated. 750,000 killed and 2.5m wounded was the grim tally for Britain and the 1914-1918 War casts a dark shadow that reaches down the years to the present time. In retrospect, it may be seen as the opening phase of nearly a century of bitter world conflict. Unluckily, the acrimony that was consequent on the war's settlement, plus the economic ravages of the mid-wars years, was the crucible for the rise of despotic Fascist regimes, especially in Germany, Italy and Spain. Nationalistic ambition and martial fervour was to the fore and, after a relatively brief and uneasy interim, Europe, indeed, the whole planet, was plunged into a ferocious war.

The United Kingdom, despite the horrors and losses of The First World War and the economic decay that had accompanied the Depression years, had still clung to something close to its premier position as the industrial and financial capital of the world, although of course the leeway between Britain and its rivals was nowhere near as great as hitherto. The Second World War was to change all that.

The rise of Adolf Hitler and his successive attempts to bring European territories within his thrall was the actual signal for the start of full-scale war again in 1939. There were, from the British standpoint, two compelling moments. The first was when France and the Low Countries were overrun by the German advance and British troops had to be evacuated from Dunkirk in May 1940. There were fateful meetings of the War Cabinet, perhaps the most important in British history. Lord Halifax, whom Winston Churchill had narrowly outmanoeuvered from being prime minister, and Neville Chamberlain, whom Churchill had just succeeded in that role, argued that Britain should sue for peace. To the diplomatic mind, the desperate situation was such that this was the conventional reaction. The two Labour Party politicians, Clement Attlee and Arthur Greenwood, sided with the new premier, and Chamberlain reluctantly changed his mind, so the United Kingdom, and the Empire, remained in the war. For a year or so, Britain stood defiantly alone against the Fascist menace of the Axis powers, Germany and Italy and their Asiatic ally, Japan. In this their 'finest hour', when, as A.J.P.Taylor affirmed, the British people 'came of age' and held out stoutly in the face of heavy aerial assault and other losses.

The second defining moment was, as the wheel turned against the German alliance in 1941, both the United States of America, its fleet attacked by Japan at Pearl Harbour, and the Union of Soviet Socialist Republics, invaded by Germany, entered the war and made it truly global. In retrospect, one may observe that this was the point where these two great nations may be defined as super-states, with their antagonism throughout the so-called 'cold war' to be the dominating international feature for most of the rest of the 20th century. The later collapse of the Soviet bloc left the USA as the undisputed world leader by the end of the century, albeit with China showing signs of presenting a major challenge as a world power.

As for the United Kingdom, the sacrifice made in World War II was shattering. Eighteen months into the war, and Britain was bankrupt, and there was to be a sense in which complete recovery was never quite accomplished. In economic terms, Britain sank from being the leading industrial and trading nation, as it had continued to be for so long, to something like fifteenth in the global pecking order by the beginning of the 21st century. Its great manufacturing industries declined. Although its record as a financial centre endured and although the UK rather grudgingly threw in its lot with the emergent European Union – a final example of 2000 years of involvement in Europe – its economy, while never impoverished, lost the old mantel of global predominance.

This was accompanied by the rapid demolition of the British Empire. For perfectly valid reasons and, despite some scary and dismal moments, carried out more equitably than was the case with other imperial powers, Britain's colonies were quickly transformed into independent states in the post-war decades. Beginning with the granting of independence to India, with the creation of the states of

India and Pakistan in 1947, there was a very fast transference of the other colonies from the imperial yoke. Having reached the apex of its size and potency about 1890, the British Empire had, apart from the much more ephemeral network of the Commonwealth, vanished within a hundred years, making it one of the most short-lived of all of history's major and many Empires.

As a coda to the imperial retreat one must also note the creation of an independent Irish republic in 1921 (which left the abrasive problem of Northern Ireland to be faced, especially in the last third of the 20th century) as well as the devolution of powers to Scotland and Wales in 1997.

The double blow – the reversal of both economic and geopolitical fortunes – left the United Kingdom as something of a second-rate power, not a third-rate one by any means, it should be added, but by no means enjoying its standing of Victorian times. Like the rest of the world it was subject to occasional sloughs of economic failure, one or two of them quite critical, although by and large, the post-1945 decades were to bring material benefits to a population of some 60m, which, by 2010, included 9m citizens of post-colonial origin or descent. Like much of the rest of the world,Britain suffered from modern social problems, such as high crime rates, many of these problems arising from a collapse in the strong community disciplines that had held good certainly from about the 1860s to the 1960s.

Possibly the worst outcome for the United Kingdom was an inability by those in government to come to terms with the reality of lost political clout. Politicians of all brands were perhaps a little too inclined to pursue foreign military ventures, especially at the behest of the United States, in areas like Korea, the Balkans, Iraq and Afghanistan, which, from one viewpoint, were not affordable. It was as if Britain could not adjust to the not displeasing model of being a sort of larger version of Denmark, with a sound economy backed by excellent public services, and, by trying to sustain its global role, fell into the trap of becoming a somewhat inferior United States.

It must be emphasised that not all was doom and gloom. For the most part, life in early 21st century Britain was, for many of its residents, pleasant enough. In a curious way, it rather resembled the situation just before and during the Roman occupation of Britain 2000 years previously. Britain then was never regarded, as some historians have suggested, as a dark and forbidding offshore island of little consequence. It was always valued as a prize by both the native population and by the Roman occupiers, although never estimated by Rome as a major player. Some of that happy medium character appertains today at what is, by no means the end, but merely just the closure of another chapter in Britain's story.

MORE BOOKS by ERIC MIDWINTER for Third Age Press
Special prices for readers of this book (by mail order). Please add 20% for UK p&p

Novel Approaches: a guide to the popular classic novel
35 novels that have stood the test of time – embeded in historical and literary commentary.   **180 pages   £5.00**

Best Remembered . . . a hundred stars of yesteryear
A galaxy of 100 stars – from radio, cinema, stage, dance hall, theatre, variety and sport – from the days before television ruled our lives.

168 pages 248mm x 178mm   £8.00

The People's Jesters: 20th Century British Comedians
Meticulously researched and vastly entertaining.

232 pages 248mm x 178mm   £8.00

The Cricketer's Progress:Meadowland to Mumbai
The Wisden Book of the Year 2011
Sweeping panorama of English & world cricket

350 pages   £10.00

I Say, I Say, I Say: The Double Act Story
. . . attractively presented account of a significant element of popular entertainment over the last hundred years or so.

150 pages   £5.00

A Voyage of Rediscovery: guide to writing your life story   **36 pages   £4.00**

Encore: a guide to planning a celebration of your life
20 pages   £2.00

The Rhubarb People . . . Midwinter's own witty & poignant
story of growing up in Manchester in the '30s.

32 pages £4.00   or audio cassette   £4.00

FULL LIST OF THIRD AGE PRESS BOOKS
at www.thirdagepress.co.uk
or SAE to 6 Parkside Gardens London SW19 5EY